The Deadliest Insect

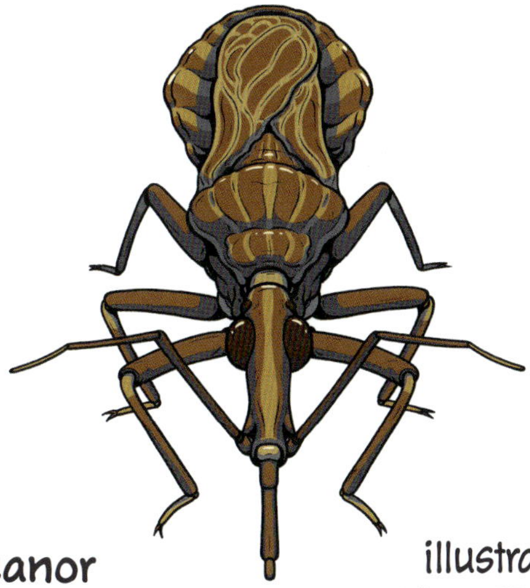

Eleanor Spicer Rice

illustrated by Max Temescu

Norton Young Readers
An Imprint of W. W. Norton & Company
Independent Publishers Since 1923

For Auston and Ione, NeeNee and Cherry –E.S.R.
For Grandpa –M.T.

Printed in Canada
First Edition

For information about special discounts for bulk purchases, please contact W. W. Norton Special Sales at specialsales@wwnorton.com or 800-233-4830

Manufacturing by Marquis
Book design by Hana Anouk Nakamura
Production manager: Delaney Adams

ISBN 978-1-324-05379-8

W. W. Norton & Company, Inc., 500 Fifth Avenue, New York, NY 10110
www.wwnorton.com

W. W. Norton & Company Ltd., 15 Carlisle Street, London W1D 3BS

1 2 3 4 5 6 7 8 9 0

WARNING!

YOU ARE ABOUT TO MEET THE DEADLIEST INSECTS ON EARTH. SOME MAY LIVE FAR AWAY. OTHERS MIGHT BE BATTING THEIR WINGS AT YOUR WINDOW SCREEN RIGHT NOW.

Two good rules for all insects, deadly or not:

1. Do not bother them. That means no stomping, grabbing, squishing, poking, or otherwise trying to make them angry. They're little! Treat a bug like you'd want a bug to treat you!

2. Do not fear them. Even if some can hurt you, all insects can delight and astound you. They help make the whole world run. Watch them! See what you find! You'll find a world of friends.

In these pages, you will meet six of the insects most feared by humans. They all hold terrifying secrets in their bodies. Only one can be crowned **THE DEADLIEST**.

WHO WILL IT BE? THE CREEPY KISSING BUG? THE NIMBLE FLEA? OR SOMEONE ELSE? LET'S FIND OUT!

THIS IS AN INSECT

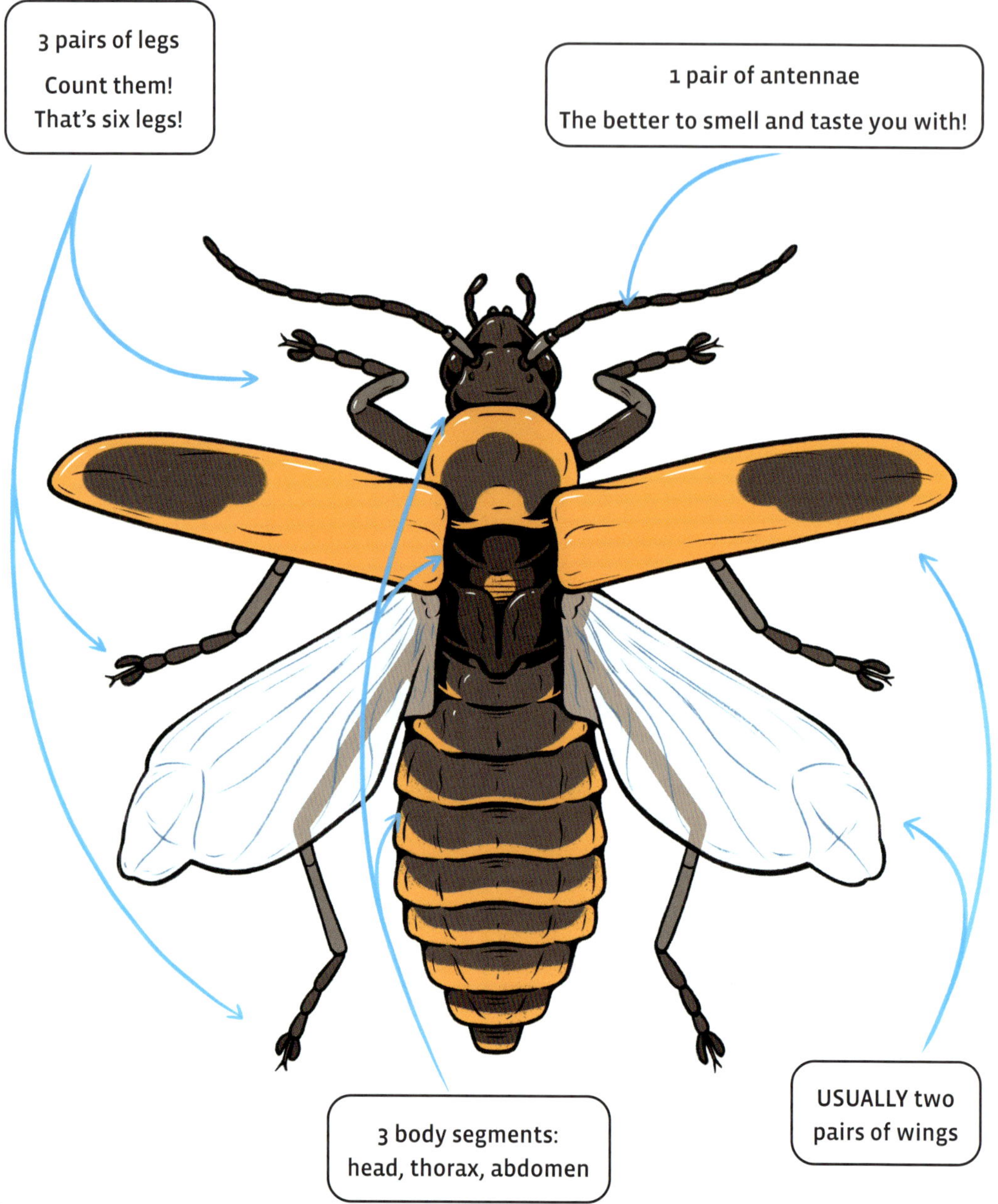

More than a million **species** of insects exist *that we know about*. Scientists think there are probably up to ten million different insect species. Most of the planet's known species are insects.

SPECIES: what scientists call one type of living thing. For example, a honey bee is one species, *Apis mellifera*. Argentine ants are another species, *Linepithema humile*.

WHO'S NOT AN INSECT?

Out of the way, folks. This book's for the six-leggers.

Many of us call all insects *bugs*, and that's okay. But a "true bug" is actually a type of insect called a hemipteran. Stink bugs and kissing bugs are hemipterans.

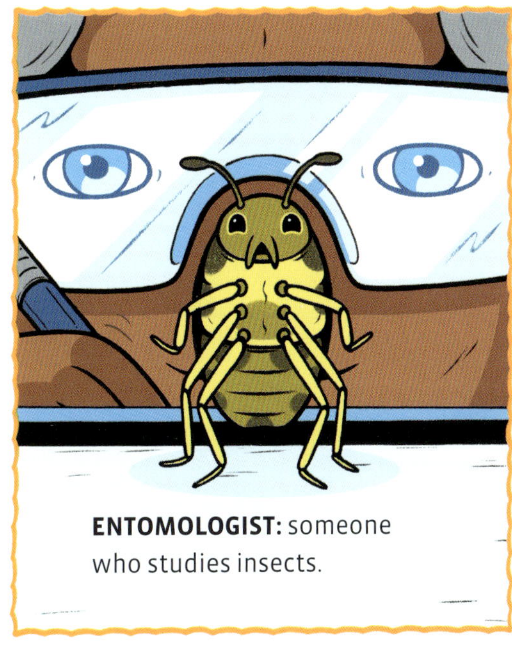

ENTOMOLOGIST: someone who studies insects.

ENTOMOPHILE: someone who loves insects (like you and me).

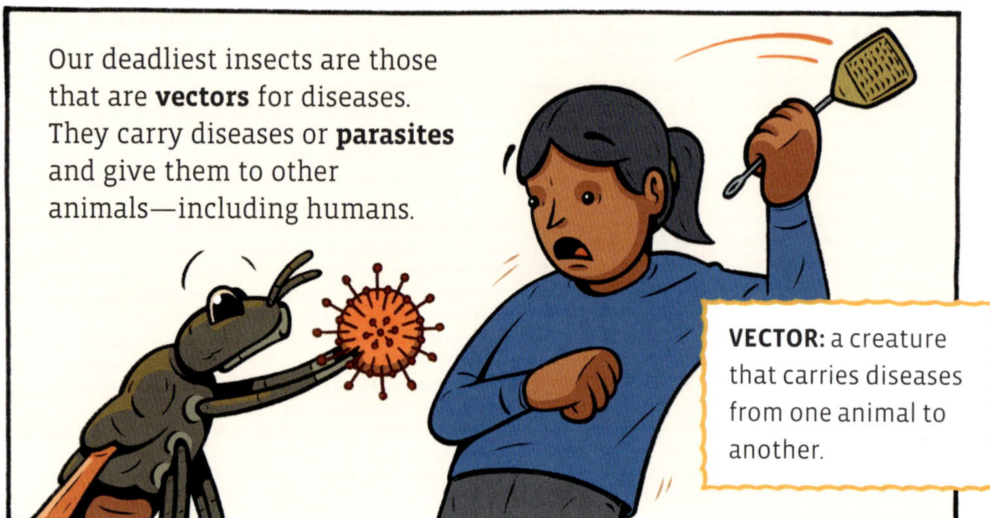

Wait . . . if some insects can give us deadly diseases, why don't we just kill them all?

Not so fast. Hold those flyswatters, people!

PARASITE: an animal that lives on or inside another animal, causing it harm.

. . . And much, much more.

ONE BIG REASON NOT TO KILL ALL THE INSECTS

Scientists think that if we killed all Earth's insects (and that would be tough because there are an estimated 200 *million* insects for every human on the planet), the planet would experience a food chain collapse.

That means all **ecosystems** on Earth would no longer be able to support life, resulting in mass extinction.

ECOSYSTEM: all the living and nonliving things in an environment and their interactions with each other. A desert, with its rocks, cacti, harvester ants, sand, and hot winds, is part of an ecosystem.

In short, without insects, we'd all be toast.

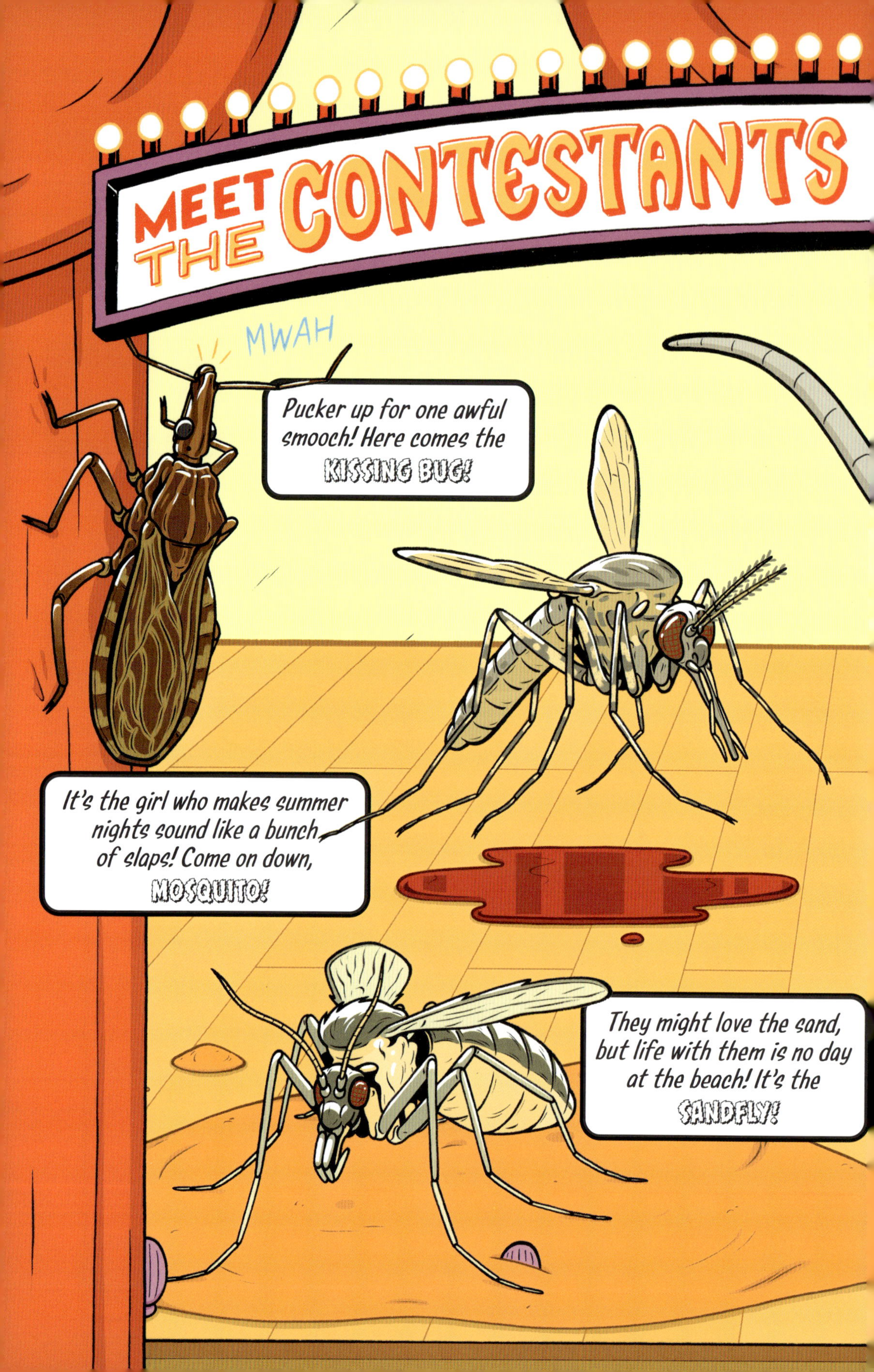
MEET THE CONTESTANTS
MWAH
Pucker up for one awful smooch! Here comes the KISSING BUG!
It's the girl who makes summer nights sound like a bunch of slaps! Come on down, MOSQUITO!
They might love the sand, but life with them is no day at the beach! It's the SANDFLY!

WHO PACKS THE DEADLIEST PUNCH?
WHO HIDES THE MOST DISASTROUS DISEASE?
FLEAS with disease? Yes, please!
Making our bodies home since 200,000 BCE! Say hello to the LOUSE!
Cute name, terrible reputation! Get down here, TSETSE FLY!
WHO WILL BE THE DEADLIEST INSECT?

We know of about 138 species of kissing bugs in the world, but five species that live in South and Central America are the deadliest.

Panstrongylus megistus

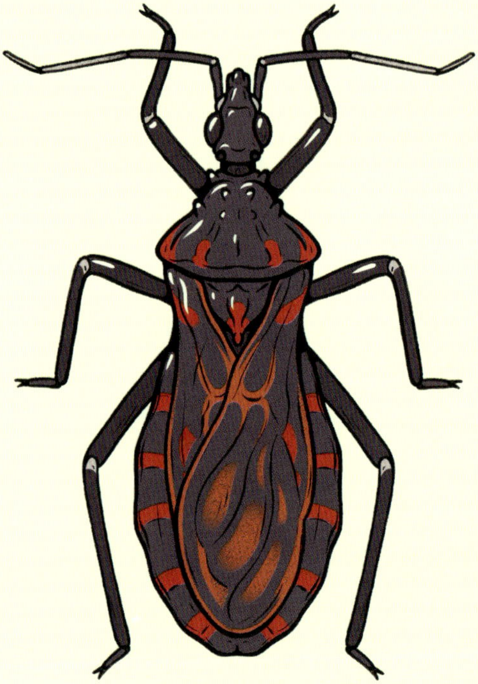

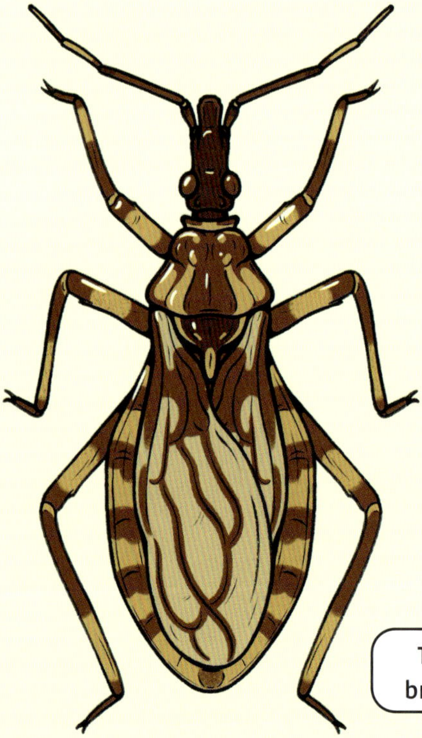

Triatoma brasiliensis

Triatoma dimidiata

Triatoma infestans

Rhodnius prolixus

Kissing bugs are the only "true bugs" on our deadliest list. That means they have:

mouths like beaks

4 wings with leathery tops folded over their backs

babies that look like grown-ups (except they don't have wings)

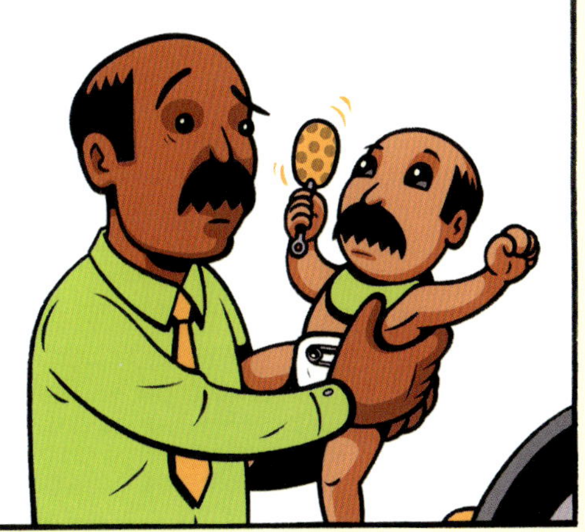

Okay, maybe lots of us don't.

If you met a kissing bug, you would HATE being kissed.

Kissing bugs like to creep up on sleeping people.

They bite us near our mouths and suck our blood.

While they bite, they poop and pee waste onto our faces.

Sleeping us says, "Something itches!" and we rub the bite mark, smearing the poop into the bite wound.

Then, the trouble begins. Some kissing bugs are infected with the parasite that causes Chagas disease.

WHAT IF YOU SMEARED A DOOKIE FULL OF PARASITES INTO YOUR FACE? WHAT WOULD HAPPEN IF YOU GOT CHAGAS?

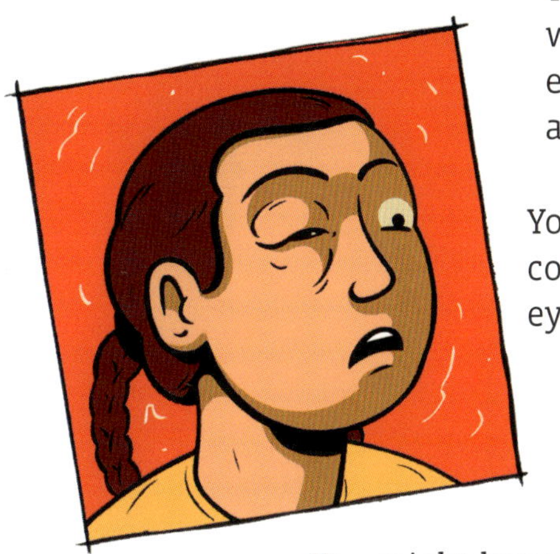

You'd have an idea something was up within a few days after the parasite entered the wound and started moving around in your blood.

You'd get a purplish-colored sore. One eyelid would swell.

You might have a fever and difficulty breathing. Your chest or belly might hurt.

Then, the horrible long haul would begin.

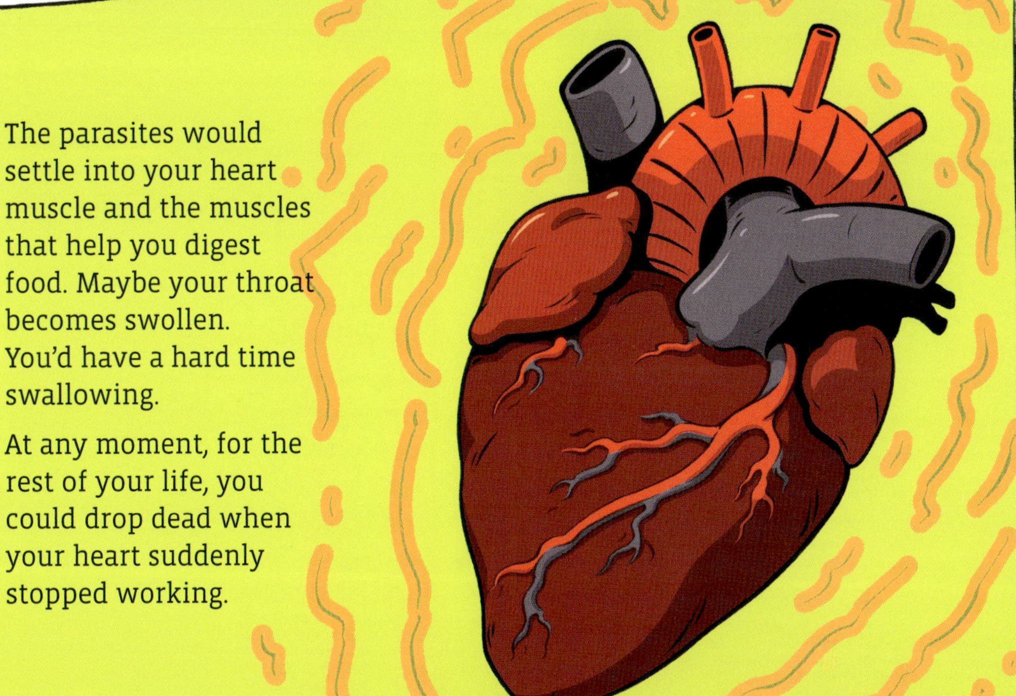

The parasites would settle into your heart muscle and the muscles that help you digest food. Maybe your throat becomes swollen. You'd have a hard time swallowing.

At any moment, for the rest of your life, you could drop dead when your heart suddenly stopped working.

THAT'S A DEADLY KISS! BUT IS IT THE DEADLIEST?

CONTESTANT NUMBER TWO

MOSQUITO

Size: *0.15–0.4 inches. About the size of the eraser on your pencil.*

Distribution: *Every continent except Antarctica*

Mosquitoes are a type of fly. Unlike most insects, flies have two full wings in the front and two smaller wings in the back that are like balls on sticks, called halteres. Halteres are for balance and help make flies nimble in the air.

Sure, it's easy to hate mosquitoes.

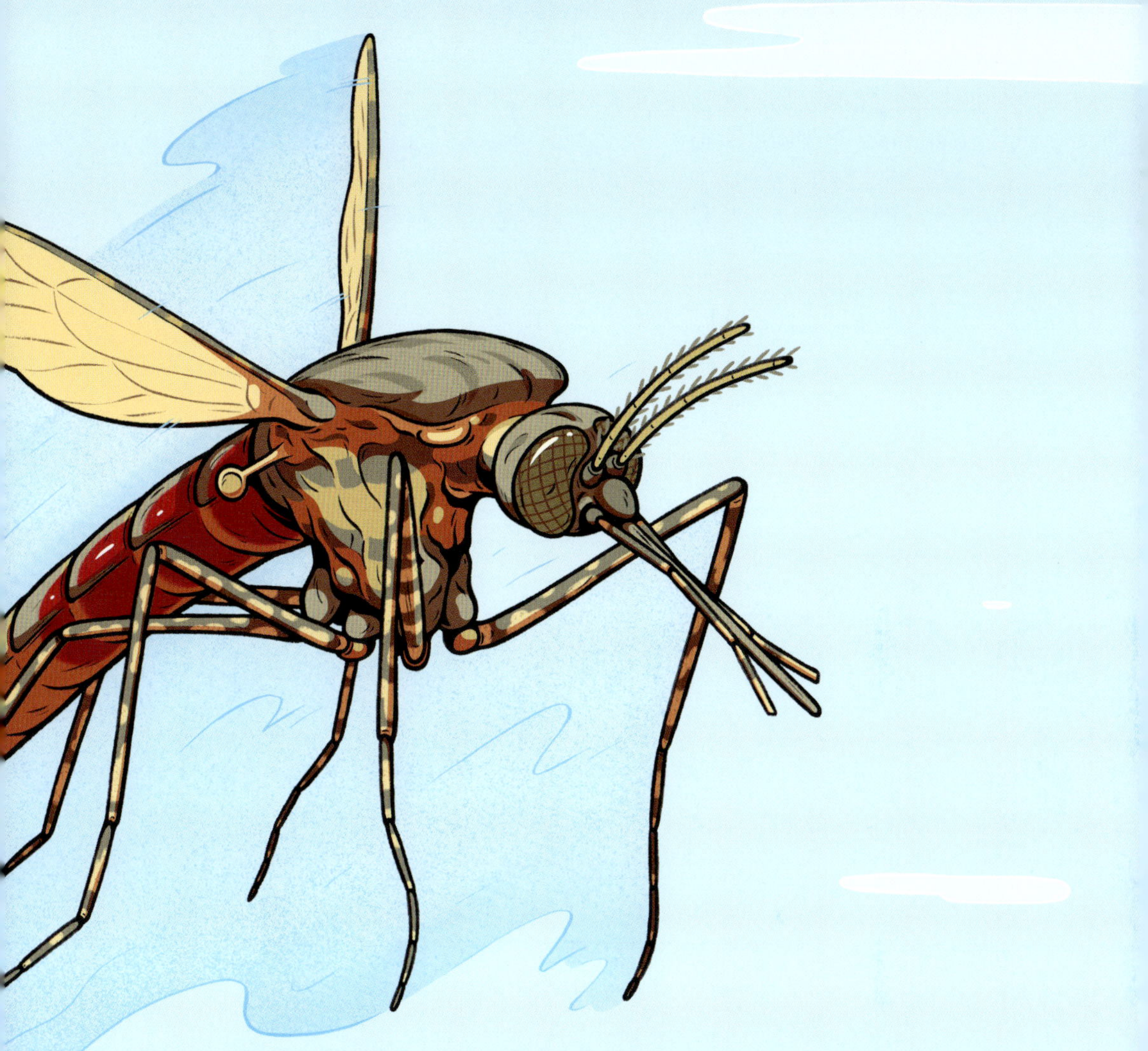

It seems like every mosquito is out to get us.

The truth is, more than 3,000 species of mosquitoes live on Earth. Fewer than 100 can make us sick. Most don't bother humans at all.

Most mosquito females need blood to feed their eggs.

Male mosquito: Fluffy antennae. Eats pollen and nectar.

Female mosquito: No fluffs on antennae. Blood-lover.

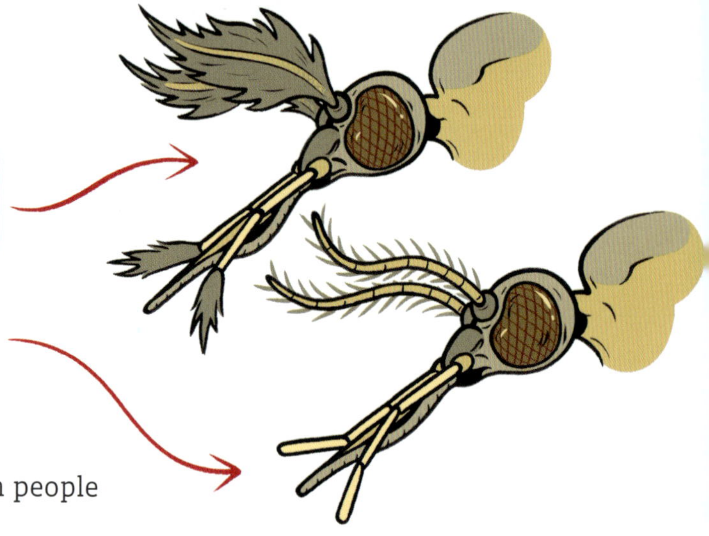

Some mosquitoes that feed on people carry diseases.

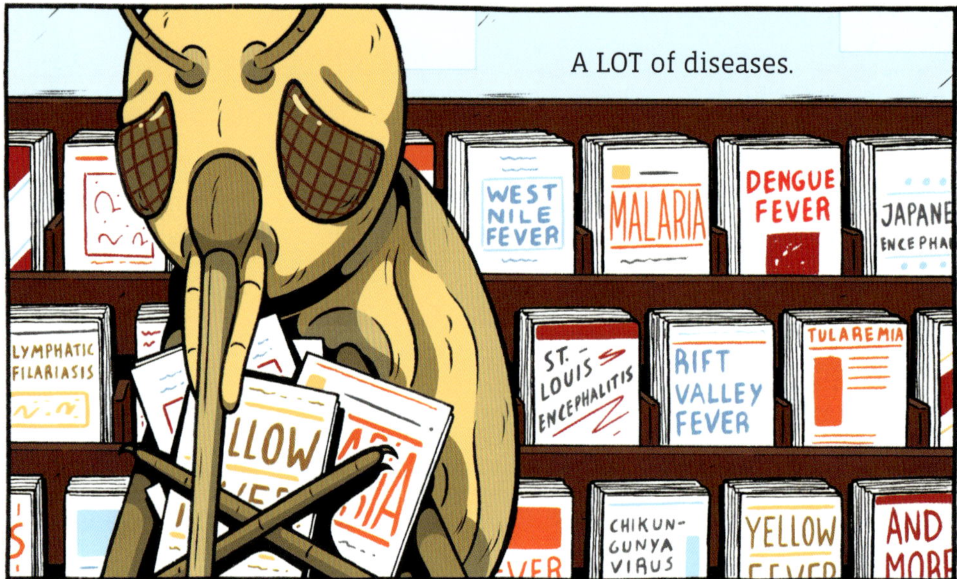

Probably the worst is malaria.

Malaria mostly lives in mosquitoes (and humans!) in Africa.

Like chagas, malaria is a parasite.

The malaria parasite makes mosquitoes sick, too.

Malaria can be treated by doctors, but it's not always easy.

WHAT IF A MALARIA-INFECTED MOSQUITO BIT YOU AND YOU COULDN'T GET TREATMENT?

At first, you might not notice anything.

In fact, you might not notice anything for a few days. You might not notice anything for *one to two years.*

All this time, malaria parasites move through your blood to your **liver**. From there, they attack your blood cells.

When that happens, you'd start feeling like you had the flu.

You'd have a fever. You'd shake. You'd have chills and a headache. You would feel exhausted.

Your body now home to millions and millions of tiny creatures, you would begin to feel sick to your stomach.

LIVER: the organ that cleans your blood and helps you digest food.

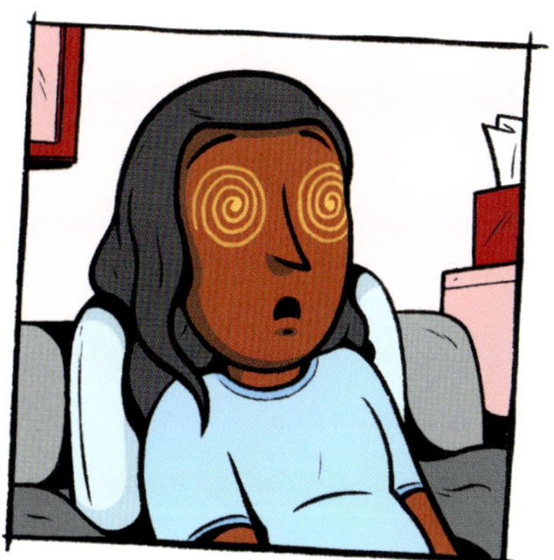

You'd become short of breath. Your organs would stop working properly.

After 10 to 15 days, malaria will have burst so many of your cells that your organs would fail.

You'd become confused, maybe slip into a coma, and fall into death.

YOU JUST TOOK THE LIVE OUT OF LIVER! BUT IS THIS **THE DEADLIEST?**

Long name, tiny killers! (Say it! *fluh-BOT-tom-us.*)

Phlebotomus sandflies are members of the more than 800 sandfly species that live all over the world. The flies that transmit the most diseases live in Bangladesh, Brazil, Ethiopia, India, South Sudan, and Sudan.

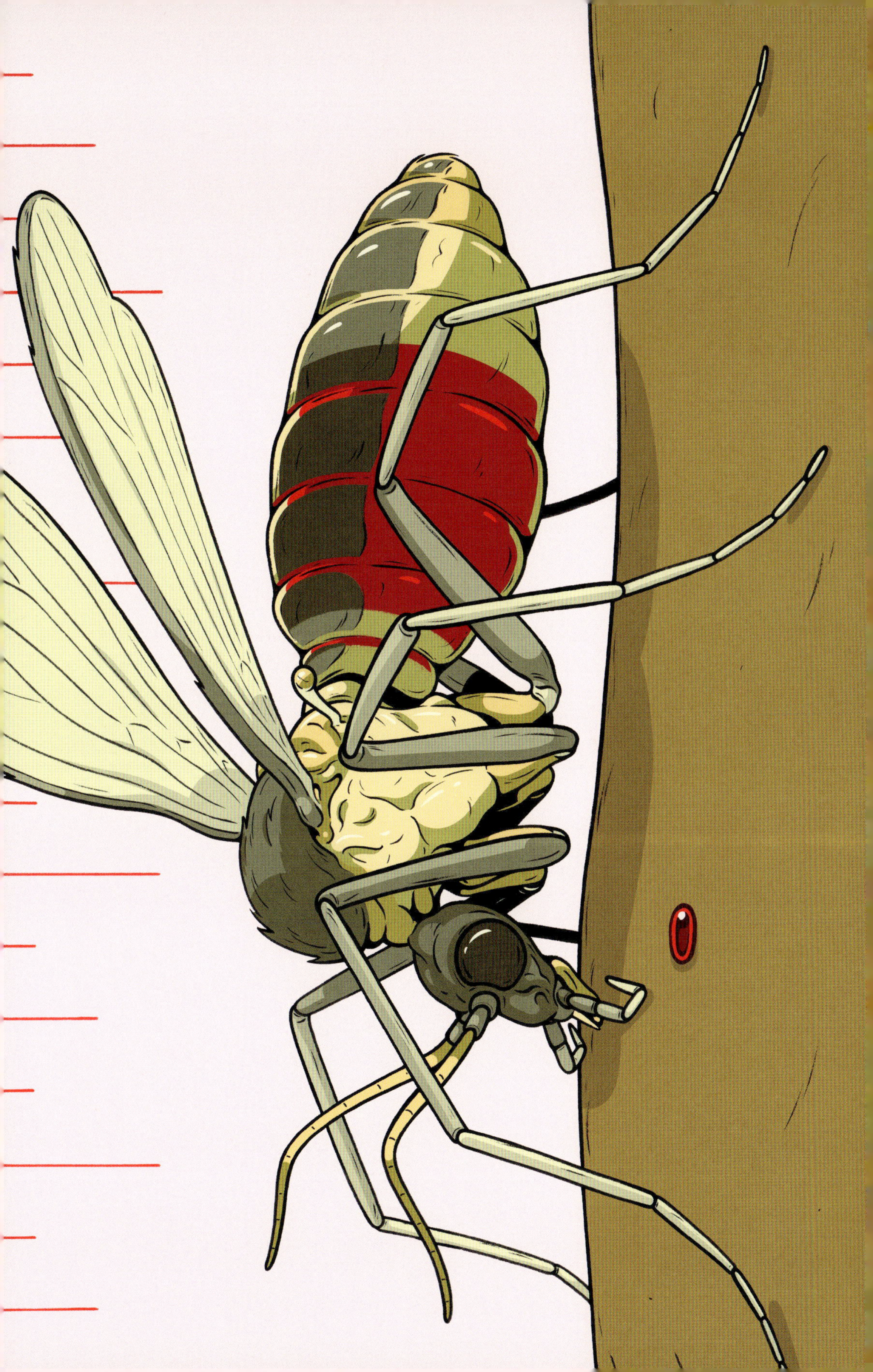

Most of the time, sandflies are pretty cute.

They eat nectar from flowers!

A little bigger than a grain of sand, you'd hardly know they were there . . .

Sandflies can stab lots of different diseases into you when they come for a meal. The worst is leishmaniasis (*leesh-mun-EYE-uh-sis*). That's a big name! Some people call it kala-azar. Some people call it black fever.

Black fever is caused by a parasite, a tiny animal with a little tail. They whip their tails around to scoot from place to place.

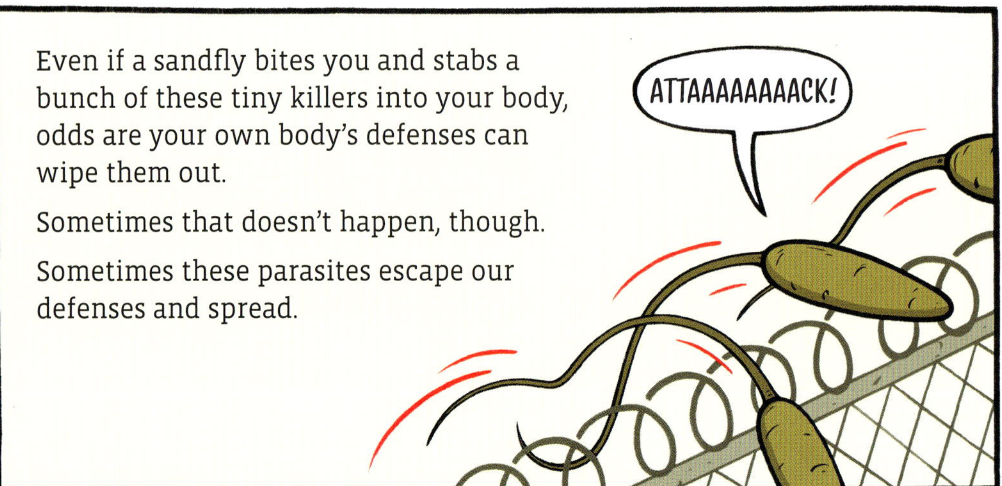

WHAT WOULD HAPPEN IF A PHLEBOTOMUS SANDFLY BIT YOU? WHAT IF YOU GOT BLACK FEVER?

In the beginning, you'd have a fever. You'd feel only a little under the weather.

Meanwhile, a small army would be breeding in your body.

It would move into your **spleen** and liver.

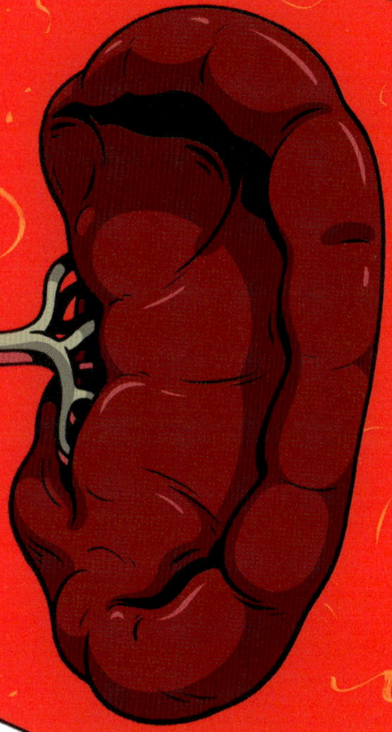

SPLEEN: an organ in your body that helps make sure your blood stays healthy

These infections would cause your body to shut down.

In as little as three months, you'd be a goner.

THAT'S A COMPLICATED WAY TO DIE! BUT IS IT THE DEADLIEST?

Fleas are tiny wingless insects that live on the bodies of all sorts of warm-blooded animals, including dogs, cats, rats, mice, birds—and sometimes humans.

There are more than 2,500 species of fleas that live on every continent, including Antarctica! Some can transmit diseases and parasites, such as typhus, cat scratch fever, and tapeworms.

One, the Oriental rat flea (*Xenopsylla cheopis*), makes our list of the deadliest.

To understand why we included this insect in the deadliest list, we need to do a bit of time travel.
All the way back about 670 years ago in Europe . . .
. . . when a flea hopped off a rat and onto a human, drank that human's blood . . .
. . . and infected them with a type of bacteria called *Yersinia pestis*, which causes the Black Death, also known as the Black Plague, Bubonic Plague, or sometimes just The Plague.
The plague spread, killing up to 200 million people in a tremendous reign of terror.
That's more than all the people who have died in human wars, combined.
Still here!
Even today, people can get the plague from fleas. It's easy to treat—but if people don't get medical care within the first day of symptoms, odds are they'll die within a week.

WHAT IF YOU WERE BITTEN BY A PLAGUE-INFESTED FLEA? WHAT IF YOU COULDN'T GET MEDICAL CARE?

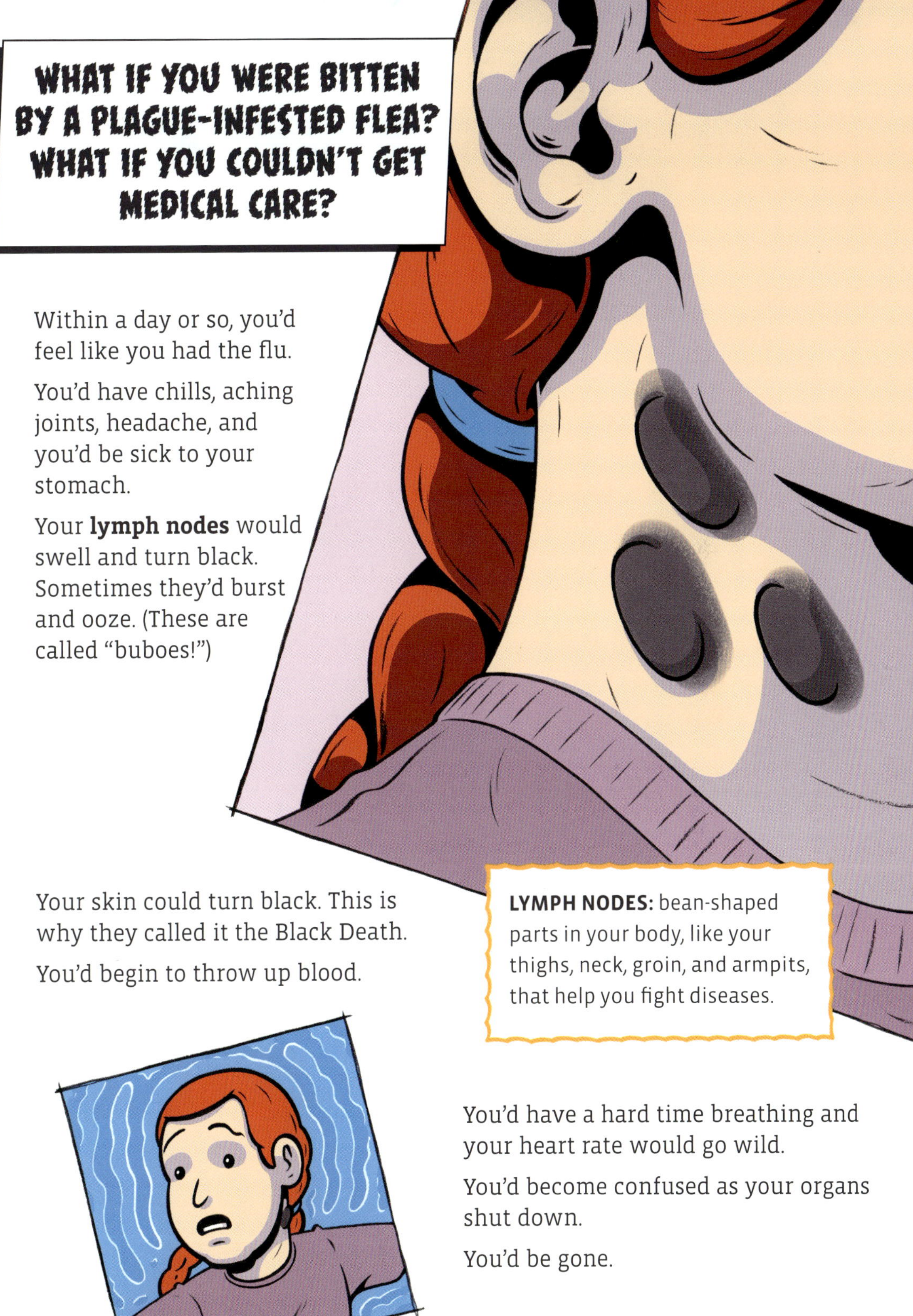

Within a day or so, you'd feel like you had the flu.

You'd have chills, aching joints, headache, and you'd be sick to your stomach.

Your **lymph nodes** would swell and turn black. Sometimes they'd burst and ooze. (These are called "buboes!")

Your skin could turn black. This is why they called it the Black Death.

You'd begin to throw up blood.

LYMPH NODES: bean-shaped parts in your body, like your thighs, neck, groin, and armpits, that help you fight diseases.

You'd have a hard time breathing and your heart rate would go wild.

You'd become confused as your organs shut down.

You'd be gone.

THAT'S CLASSIC DEADLY! BUT IS IT **THE DEADLIEST?**

CONTESTANT NUMBER FIVE
BODY LOUSE
Size: Up to 0.14 inch. Like the flea, about the size of a sesame seed.
Distribution: Wherever humans normally live

Like fleas, lice have no wings and can't fly. Human body lice (*Pediculus humanus humanus*) are passed from person to person through contact.
More than 2,600 known lice species crawl on the planet. Two of those prefer humans to all other animals. Head lice stick to your head. Body lice can scoot around all over your body.
A louse is one.
Lice is a bunch.

Lice's flat bodies make it easy for them to crawl around on us, sucking our blood, pooping, and making us itch.

The body louse carries diseases like typhus, trench fever, and relapsing fever, which it can give to us if it makes us its home. Scratching smashes the louse and rubs the bacteria into our skin.

Every now and then, such as in places that are disrupted by war, people aren't able to wash their clothes or take baths.

To make matters worse, these places are also often where people can't get medical care if they're sick, so treatable diseases become deadly ones.

WHAT IF YOU LIVED IN A WAR-TORN COUNTRY? WHAT IF YOU WERE HOSTING A RELAPSING FEVER LICE PARTY?

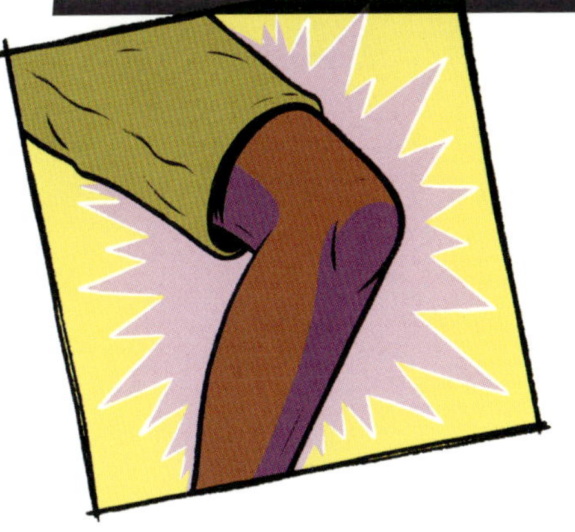

You would suddenly have a fever and get chills and headaches.

You would feel like you didn't care about anything, including eating.

Your joints and muscles would hurt.

A rash of tiny, round spots would cover your body.

You'd shake, sweat, and feel weak.

You would be exhausted and confused as the bacteria multiplied in your organs and bloodstream.

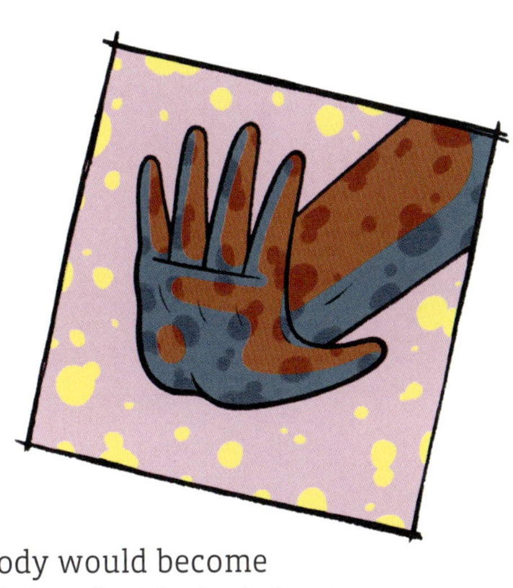

Your body would become overwhelmed with the infection. You would shut down.

THAT'S ONE DEADLY PARTY. BUT IS IT **THE DEADLIEST?**

CONTESTANT NUMBER SIX

TSETSE FLY

Size: *0.25–0.6 inch. About the size of a lima bean.*
Distribution: *Tropical Africa*

Tsetse (say it! *TSET-see!*) flies are big for flies. They're about the size of lima beans. Flying, blood-sucking lima beans. That are not good for you.

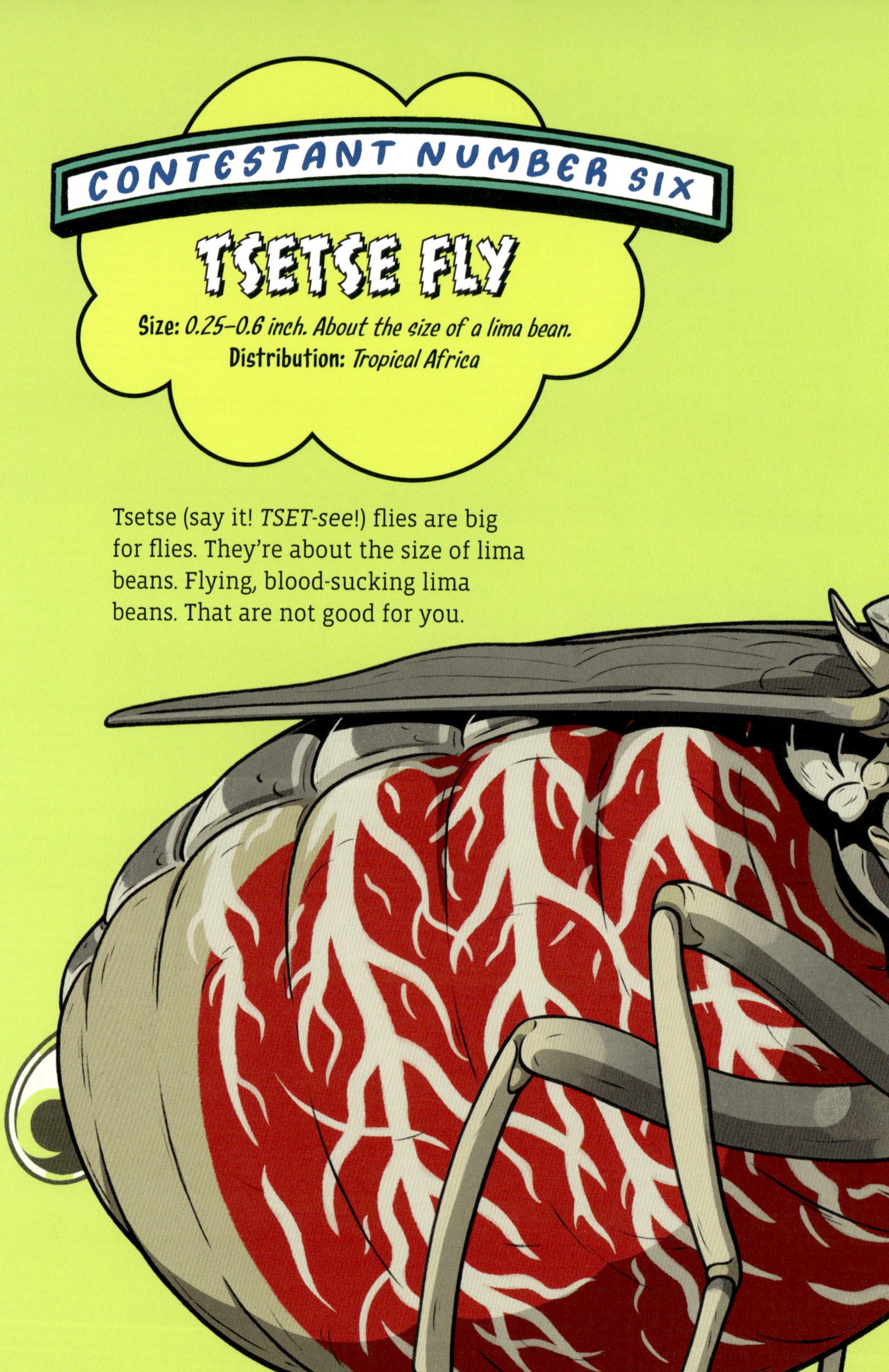

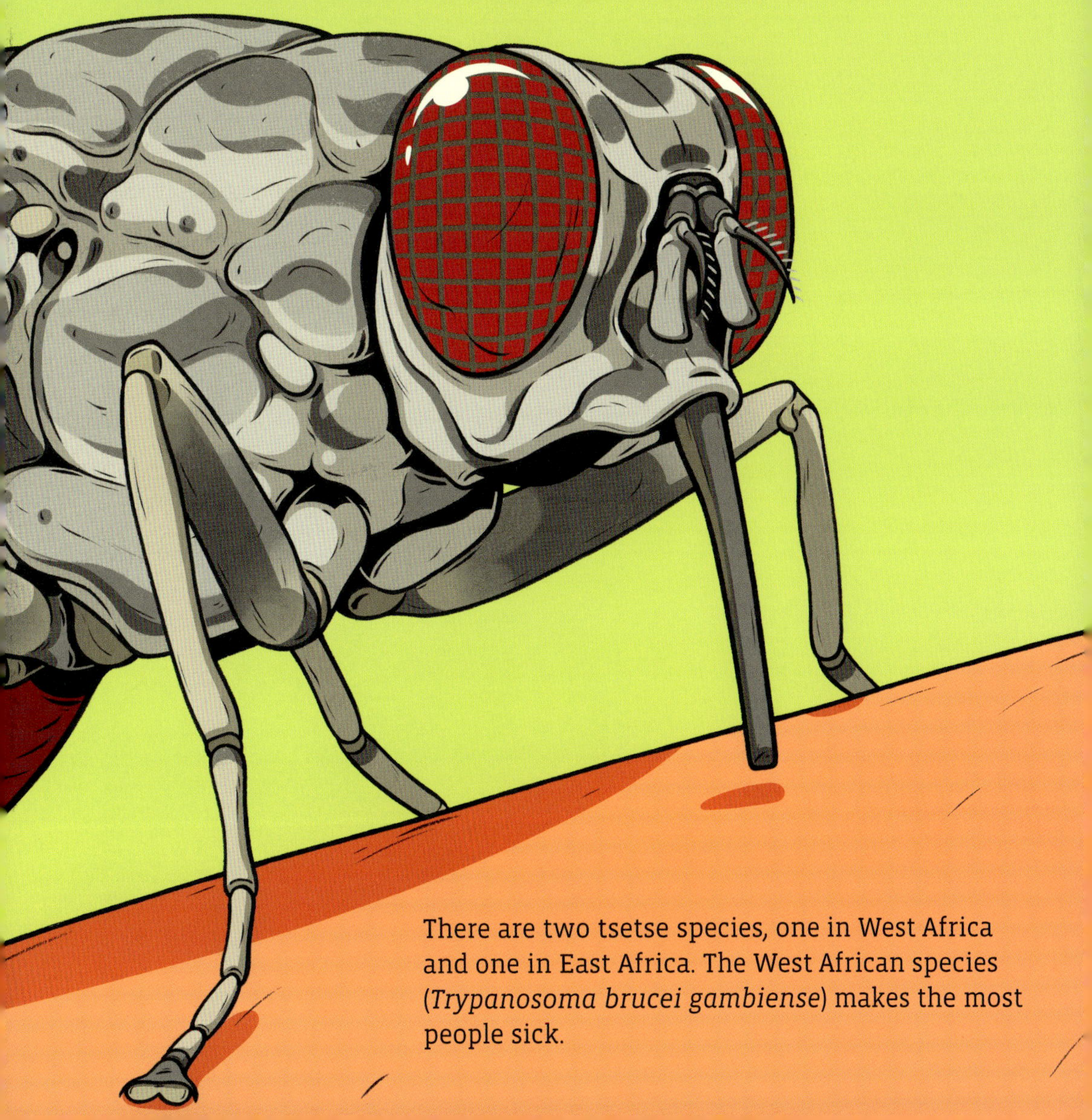

There are two tsetse species, one in West Africa and one in East Africa. The West African species (*Trypanosoma brucei gambiense*) makes the most people sick.

Some tsetse flies are infected with a parasite that causes sleeping sickness.

That's when tsetse flies go from being annoying to being deadly. When the fly bites you, it can leave behind the sleeping sickness parasite . . .

. . . which starts multiplying in your body.

WHAT WOULD HAPPEN IF AN INFECTED TSETSE FLY BIT YOU? WHAT IF YOU COULDN'T GET HELP?

Immediately, you would:
notice an ulcer forming at the bite site right away.

In a week or two, you would:
get a headache,
feel weak, exhausted, itchy, and your joints would hurt.

In a year or so, the fevers go away!

But you're really sick now. You:

lie awake all night and sleep all day,

start to **hallucinate**,

feel anxious and cry,

get confused, can't pay attention,

start speaking in a weird way,
feel like pins and needles are prickling you,

have a hard time seeing.

Then, you'd fall into a coma.
You get to nap. Forever!

HALLUCINATE: seeing things that aren't there.

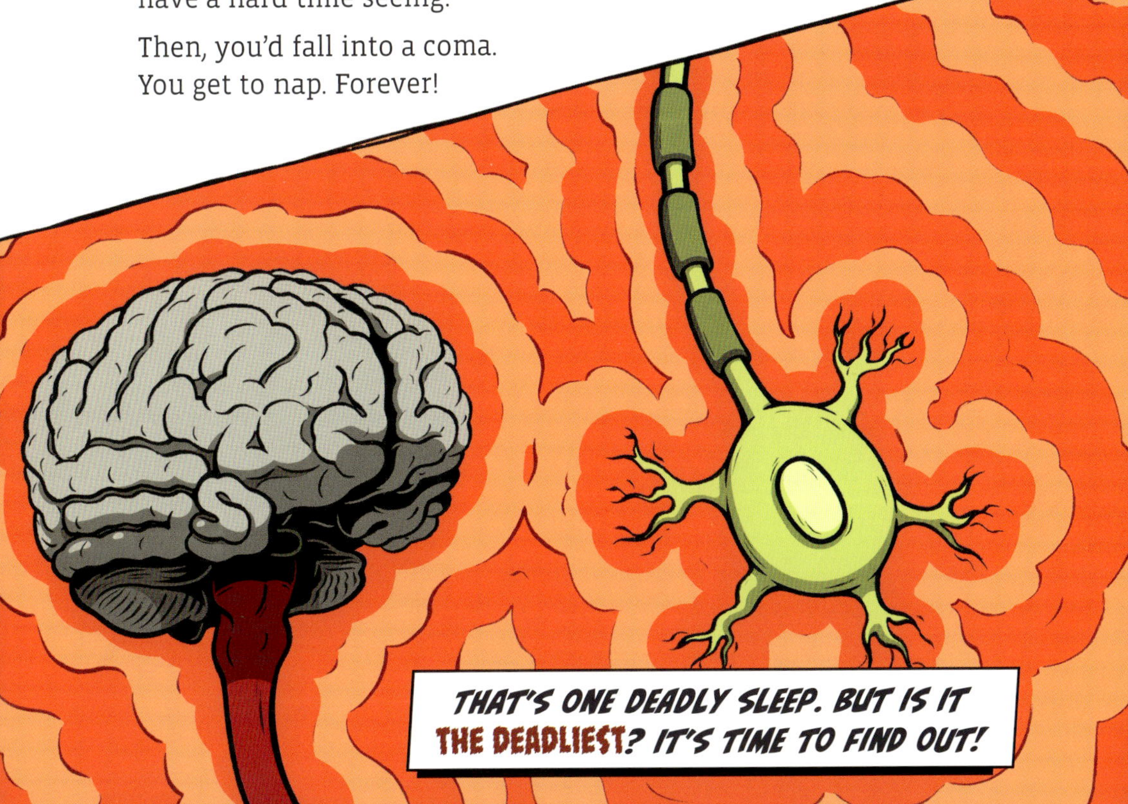

THE DEATH-O
PHLEBOTOMUS SANDFLY
Average number of humans killed each year: 20,000–40,000
MOSQUITO
Average number of humans killed each year: 650,000
KISSING BUG
Average number of humans killed each year: 10,000
WHAT'S THE BIG DEAL?
WOW! THAT HURT
DEFINITELY GOING TO THE HOSPITAL

METER

FLEA
Average number of humans killed each year: fewer than 1,000

BODY LOUSE
Average number of humans killed each year: up to a few thousand

TSETSE FLY
Average number of humans killed each year: more than 1,000

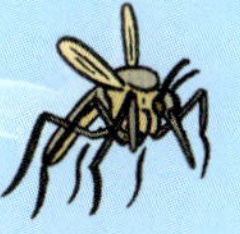

WHO IS THE DEADLIEST INSECT?

YOU MIGHT DIE

DEATH IS LIKELY

SAY GOODBYE

IN THIS BITEY BATTLE, THE DEADLIEST INSECT IS ...
THE MOSQUITO!
But mosquitoes bite me all the time and I'm still around!
Of course you are. Even though the number of people who die as a result of mosquito bites is very high, the odds of dying from a mosquito bite are very low.
You'd have to spend lots of time in places where malaria and other diseases carried by mosquitoes flourish.
And not have the proper prevention.
And not be able to get treatment.

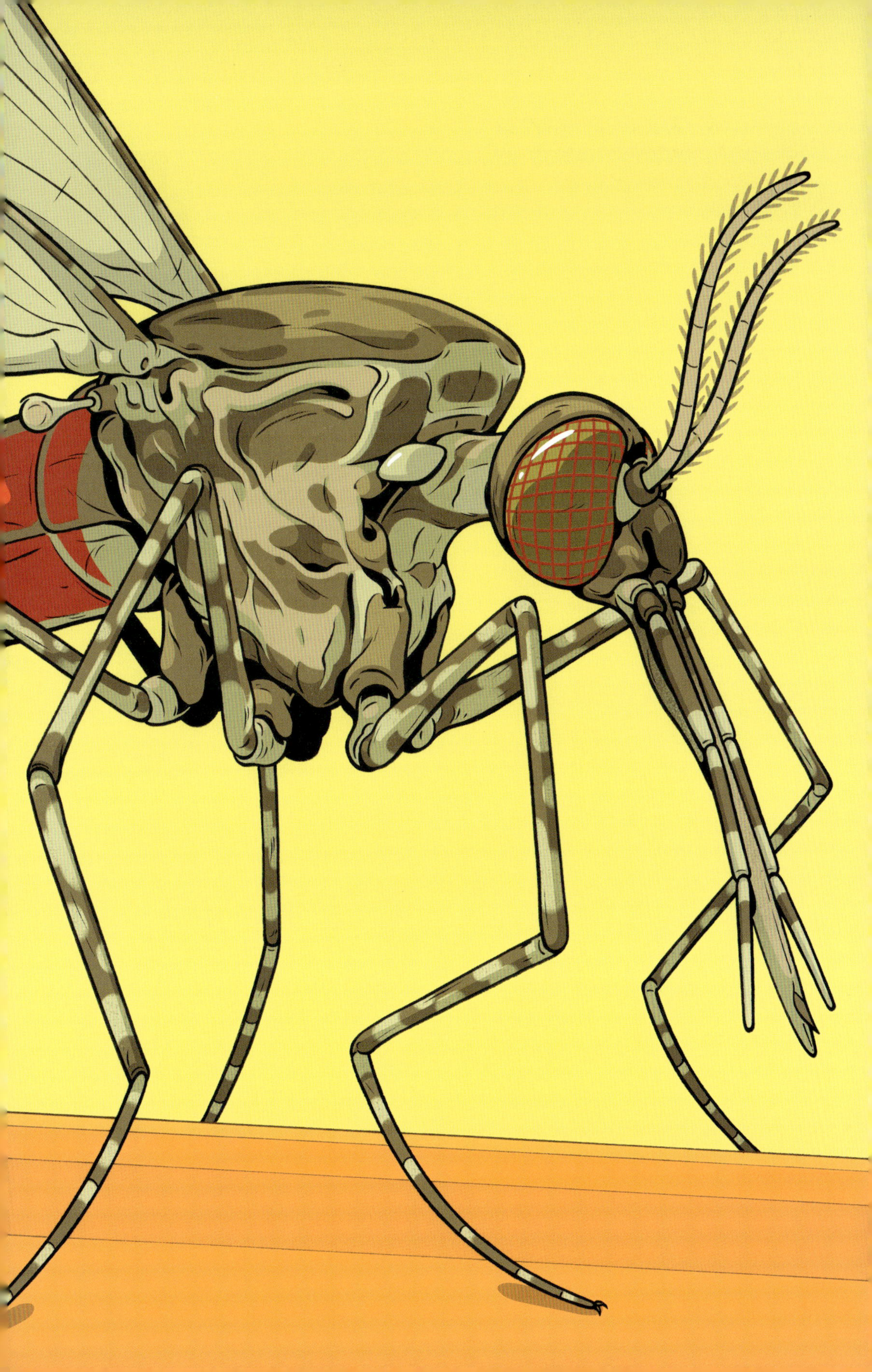

Mosquitoes alone kill way more humans than deadly snakes, big cats, sharks, hippos, car crashes, falling coconuts, angry dogs, wolves, cattle stampedes, and bee stings *combined*.

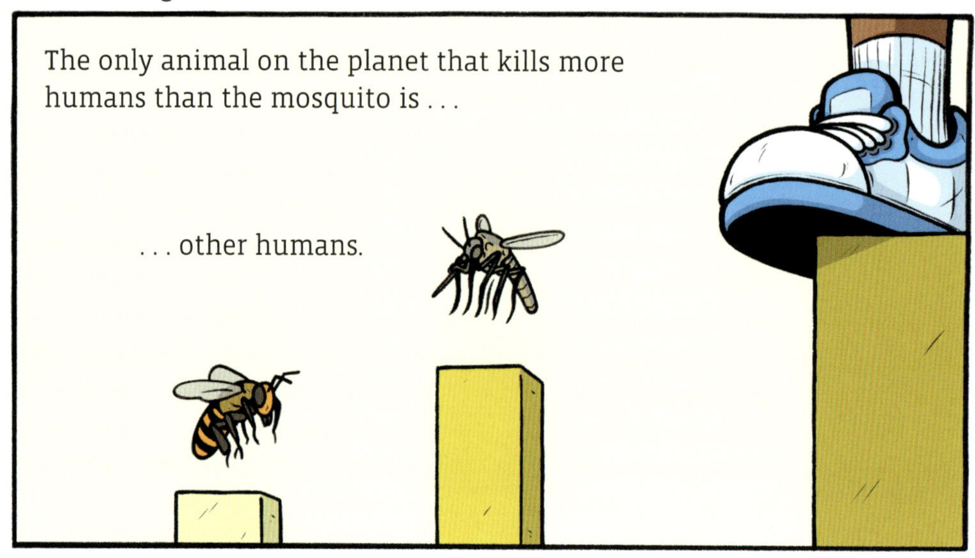

REMEMBER!

These are six of the deadliest insects on the planet, but they're not the only dangerous insects.

And even though some can hurt us, insects are truly essential to making our planet function. They pollinate the plants we depend on for food, keep soil healthy, feed countless other species of animals, and much more.

We need them all, doing their jobs. Each job might be tiny . . .

. . . but they add up . . .

ULTIMATE DEADLY

Each of these deadly insects has its own superpowers. Combine them to create your own Ultimate Deadly creature! Use these superpowers we found, or discover more and use those!

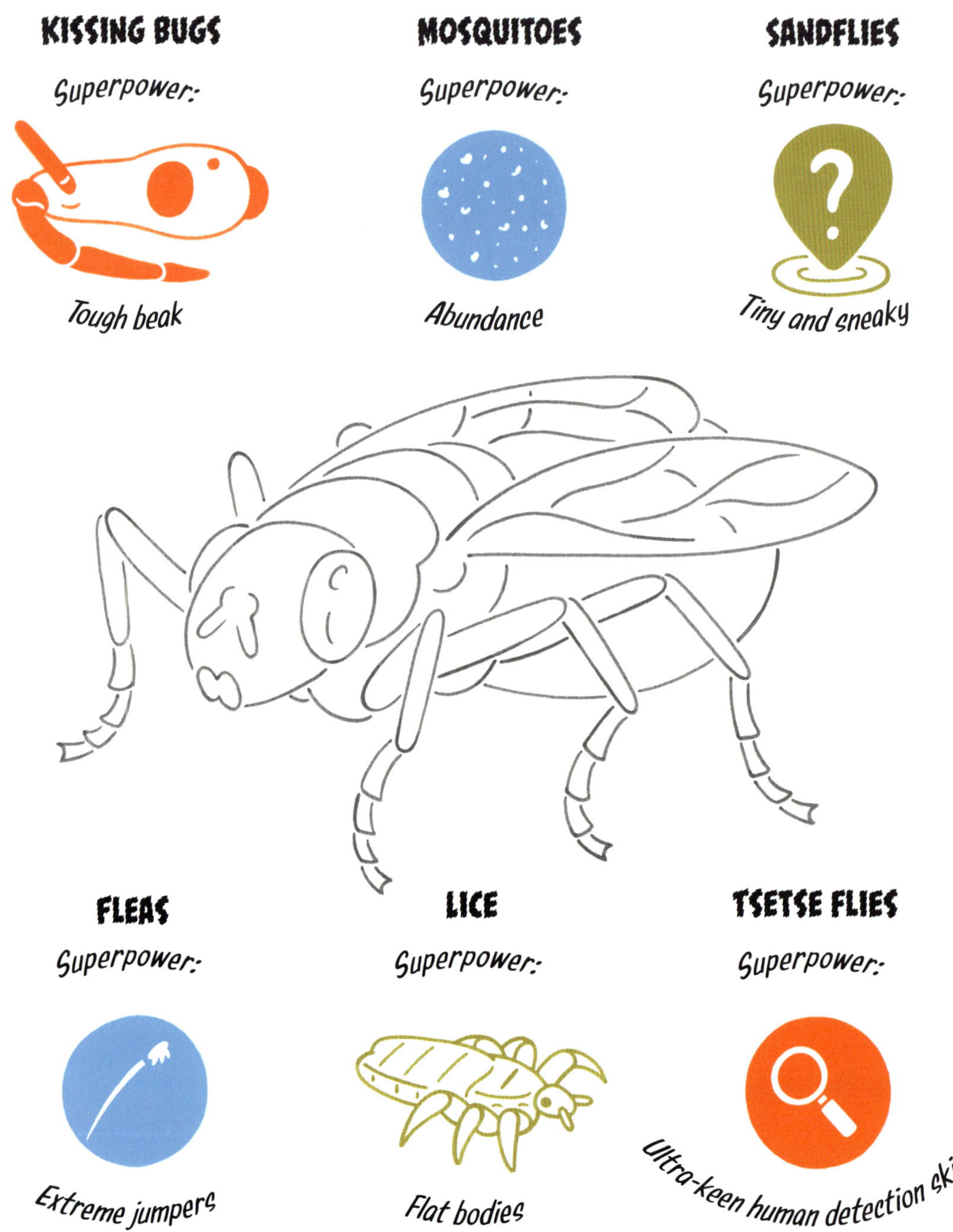